the souls
I GAVE AWAY

ONE WOMAN'S STORY OF
ABORTION AND GOD'S GRACE

DEBORAH KIRK

innovo
PUBLISHING

Published by Innovo Publishing, LLC
www.innovopublishing.com
1-888-546-2111

innovo
PUBLISHING

Providing Full-Service Publishing Services for Christian Authors, Artists & Ministries:
Books, eBooks, Audiobooks, Music, Film & Courses

THE SOULS I GAVE AWAY
One Woman's Story of Abortion and God's Grace

*Although the stories in this book are true, all names and identifying details have been changed to
protect the privacy of individuals.*

Unless otherwise noted, all scripture is taken from the King James Version (KJV)
of the Bible.

THE HOLY BIBLE, NEW INTERNATIONAL VERSION®, NIV® Copyright
© 1973, 1978, 1984, 2011 by Biblica, Inc.® Used by permission. All rights
reserved worldwide.

Library of Congress Control Number: 2019907613
ISBN: 978-1-61314-477-0

Cover Design & Interior Layout: Innovo Publishing, LLC

Printed in the United States of America
U.S. Printing History
First Edition: 2019

In Memory of and Dedication to:

My mother was a country girl and tough as nails. The Lord Jesus, Momma, and my daughters, Frances and Melanie, gave me the drive to push through all obstacles, small and large. My mother-in-law, Sally Lou, was my spiritual angel, followed by today's angel on earth, Patricia. These five women are the inspiration for my love of life and of Jesus Christ our Savior. I miss my mother and mother-in-law, who are in the arms of the Lord in Heaven already. Not a day goes by that I don't think of my dear momma and her encouraging words.

Each of us have angels in our life. Some are visible; some are not. If we open our hearts, we can feel their presence around us and experience their soothing comfort. These women are just five of mine, and I shall always cherish them.

Endorsements

"Some authors write good things. Other authors are good writers. Sometimes both are found in one. Deborah Kirk has written some good things: They are *real* things; they are *life* things; they are *hard* things; they are *humorous* things. Furthermore these things are well written. Deborah has courageously invited the reader into her life. Not only has she addressed one of the most volatile issues in our culture, but she has done so transparently. Not an armchair quarterback but a fully involved (and bruised) player on the field. Deborah speaks with candor and brokenness regarding her abortions, broken marriages, poor choices, and the remarkable forgiveness and restoration from Jesus. I believe this book will be a ministry as well as a preventive to many who read it."

—Dr. Dan Robinson, Highlands Central Baptist Church, Highlands, North Carolina

"A triumph of truth and grace. In this thought-provoking book, Debbie compellingly tells her story in a way that moves the reader into action. The book demonstrates the triumph of the grace of God over sin, forgiveness over self-hatred, and truth over falsehood. It offers a profound encouragement to all who are haunted by past wrong decisions and makes a strong case for the inclusion of God, from whom human beings derive their existence and meaning, in our ethical decisions and choices. This is a very important book for our time! I strongly recommend this book to all those who seek to reconcile themselves to their true selves."

—Father Emmanuel Osigwe, Ph.D., Parochial Vicar, St. Mary's Church, Breckenridge, Colorado

"I met Deborah Kirk in 2010, and she is truly one who cares about God and people. Since knowing Deborah, I have watched the Word of God change the way she sees this world (Romans 12:2). So many people and even Christians determine the values and view of life by their own personal experiences and emotions. I believe the writing of her story has no personal ambition involved. She truly wants to tell her story to help hurting women and detour others from the pain she has experienced. (ref: 2 Corinthians 1:3-4)."

— Pastor Daniel Green, Eastland Baptist Church, Orlando, Florida

Contents

Preface

$\mathcal{G}$od told me to write this book one evening in early 2018 at the cabin in North Carolina. It was a beautiful spring day with the rhododendron, hydrangeas, and mountain laurel in full bloom—a carpet of pink, white, and red with an occasional blue hydrangea peeking through the maze of colors. My eyes popped wide open, and I gasped for air as I realized fully what He said. My sweet little puppy dog, Tommy, resting at my feet, woke up and looked at me suspiciously.

I did not want to write this book. I did not want to lay out my sins for everyone to see, judge, and criticize. Even though the Scripture says, "For all have sinned and fall short of the glory of God" (Rom. 3:23), it was much easier to keep those selfish actions from the past safely hidden in that "personal" folder for my eyes only. You see, in my earlier years, my twenties and thirties, I was very self-centered, determined, and focused. While these can be very positive attributes, they can also be negative in nature, especially when you don't keep the Lord front and center as your moral compass.

I was humbled by God's directive and knew I had to comply. I understood fully that there would be negative consequences with family, friends, and professional colleagues with the disclosure of my past actions. As a remnant of God's people, I will be judged one day on my actions or lack of actions to help others. I just had to relinquish my control to Him, which is much easier said than done.

When I found myself pregnant and faced with an unwanted pregnancy, I did not fully grasp the magnitude of that precious life growing inside of me, and I was not counseled about the marvelous blessing that child would be to everyone and especially to me, the mother. Yes, I already had two young daughters, but not being raised in the church, or even having received a school lesson on pregnancy, their presence was simply the outcome of follies with their father. Even the military hospitals where they were born simply provided the mechanics of the delivery service. I loved my daughters, but in those early years, I didn't understand the God-given miracle of their birth, their special placement in my life, or how they would always be a true blessing to me and many others. Later in life, God gave me the wisdom to understand the true gift of my two daughters and showed me how they had saved me.

Abortion clinics do not help you understand the miracle growing inside of you. Scripture says, "Before I formed you in the womb I knew you" (Jer. 1:5), but the clinics do not counsel the mother based upon this Scripture, and they do not provide abortion alternatives to the mother—options such as adoption, allowing other family members to raise the child, or even allowing the father to raise the child. But most of all, pregnant women are not warned of the psychological effects of abortion: the devastating effects in the years to come, knowing that you have killed your child and thus lack that whole lineage of joy in your life. You lack their smiles and participating in their achievements; you lack the joy of the grandchildren you might have held.

Women tend to keep the aborted pregnancy confidential, and their actions can be a source of shame and embarrassment for the rest of their lives. Even if that shame and embarrassment is never shared with another, it will eat them up like a cancer from the inside. Their hearts will ache for that child. It is only by the grace of God, His son Jesus, and with His forgiveness, that a person like me can live with what I did.

With God's guidance in writing this true story, I hope I can positively influence the lives of women of all ages who, like me, are dealing with the psychological effects of an abortion, and help those young women who may be considering killing their babies consider the options instead. My decision to kill my babies was complex, influenced by the powerful drive to be independent and self-sufficient, the desire to strive in a man's world, and the need to protect and support the children I had already birthed at a very young age. This book will lead you through the pressures, experiences, emotions, and consequences of those decisions in my life—and most importantly, will celebrate the grace of God, which allowed me to forgive myself.

The story starts in the year 1972 when I was in high school in Charleston, South Carolina. I hope my experiences will make you smile, laugh, cry, and maybe realize how the decisions we make can have far-reaching consequences. God is forgiving and accepting of you and me with all our flaws and sins. The Bible tells us that, "For God so loved the world that he gave his one and only Son (Jesus), that whoever believes in him shall not perish but have eternal life" (Jn. 3:16). This promise holds true no matter how dark or devastating our sin.

Momma

My story really begins with my mother's story. Momma was born June 29, 1932, in Canon, Georgia, which is, as the crow flies, an hour and a half north of Atlanta. The area is primarily farm country and the foothills of the Smoky Mountains. In Canon, they raised cows, pigs, chickens, cotton, and watermelon, and families grew their own vegetables every year in the Georgia red clay. Momma was the seventh child of ten born to an Irish farmer, Perry, and a stay-at-home mom, Elizabeth. Times were very different from today, with World War II and the Great Depression making life a matter of survival. People lived off the land, and no handouts were available except what your dear neighbor might provide. Bartering between neighbors for food, animals, and services was common. Fresh ham shanks hung in the smokehouse, and food was canned and stored each year in the cellar. It was a hard life for my grandparents as they struggled to feed a large family and stay warm, just hoping to make enough money farming to pay the taxes and the land payment.

In Georgia at that time, high school graduation was at the end of the tenth grade, and Momma finished two years ahead of the others. At fifteen, she was a bartender at the local pub, closing the business for the owner late each night. She was a very intelligent, proud, determined young woman, making a few dollars to help the family and maybe buy some fabric to make herself a new dress or blouse. She was a tall, thin, dark-haired woman with dark brown eyes. Her cotton dress was snug at her thin waist and showed off her tall, slim figure. Later in life, she kept her fingernails filed like sharp knives at a point so she could pierce our hand or arm when any of us children got out of line.

Momma met my father, Thomas, in Canon and married him in 1953. He was a handsome young sailor who had grown up just a few miles from her home. Two years later, on March 27, 1955, I was born in Charleston, South Carolina, where Daddy was stationed at the time. Momma loved Folly Beach, just south of Charleston, where they rented a small cabin one block from the ocean. It was so different from the nasty red clay hills of north Georgia and that God-forsaken country life. At least that's the way she told it. In the summer heat back home, you had to pick strawberries, cotton, and watermelon. In the cool of the evening or early in the morning, you had to feed the pigs, collect the eggs from the hen house, and help Mother in the kitchen. My daddy was her passage out of that small, gossipy, country bumpkin town called Canon. At Folly Beach, as far as you could see north and south, were the warm, sandy, white beaches. The salt air in her nostrils, the sand and seashells under her feet, and the gulls in the air all came together to form the best days she would have with my father.

The birth of my brothers and a sister followed in quick succession. In January 1960, when my little sister was born, the birth control pill was introduced. The last pregnancy, and the birth of my little sister, almost killed my mother. The doctor said, "No more babies." So, Daddy got a vasectomy. I suspect that was not a difficult decision for him since he was such a ladies' man. He loved to drink and party, and he loved women. Momma, surrounded by four children, with only a high school diploma and minimal job skills—other than briefly bartending, housekeeping, and sewing—was trapped in a marriage with an abusive husband. I would learn later that marriage did not have to be a horrible, abusive experience.

In the 1950s, 60s, and 70s, divorce was not normally an option. Momma could not take her children and go back to Georgia and my grandmother's home. There just wasn't room or monies to feed everyone. So, she endured the abuse until her divorce in 1978 after her children were grown and out on their own. Daddy had retired from the Navy at that point and spent most of his time on the road. I helped as much as possible with the lawyer and expenses, but the true blessings were that the lawyer secured a good alimony payment, the small home was almost paid off, and the US Government had changed the laws to allow a wife like Momma, who had spent twenty-five years with my Dad while he was in the service, to have the benefit of medical and drug prescription coverage through TRICARE. Thank you, Jesus!

Momma stood tall through all the physical and mental abuse handed down to her though the years from my dad. She did not run. She did not hide. She taught me to seek security and independence. She taught me to stand on my own and to seek financial security so I would never be trapped by a man in an abusive relationship. She taught me to put my children first, like she did. I believe if she had not been there to take the physical and mental abuse from Dad, it would have been directed at her children. She was my savior at that time, protecting me, my brothers, and my sister from evil, including my very own father. Throughout my young life at home with Momma, I observed the abuse, and, when I could not take him punching her, his screaming, and her crying anymore, I would stand between him and her. Usually it was my screaming and crying that would bring him briefly to his senses from his drunken state of meanness, and he would stop. At least for that evening.

Momma said whatever I desired could be mine if I worked hard. I understood from her that I had to depend on myself for happiness, security, and independence. I was to create my own life, opportunities, and successes. I knew early on, in the 1970s, that I would need to fight for equal opportunity, including equal pay. And I did. Much to her satisfaction. From the time I got into the work force in Mobile, Alabama, in 1976, until she died in 2012, she encouraged, mentored, and blessed me each day of my life.

Momma believed in God. She was a member of a small Methodist church in Canon, Georgia, but I would not say she was religious. She and her siblings, at very young ages, would walk about half a mile down the country red clay road in front of Grandpa and Grandma's to Bridge Road and the church. All the family dogs, and sometimes the chickens, would follow them to church and back. I remember Momma telling me when I was young that God would destroy the earth by fire one day. I had not been to church, had not read the Bible, so what she said made no sense to me. Today the little, red brick Methodist church is where Grandma and Grandpa are buried.

It was my mother-in-law, Mrs. Simpson, who sparked the love of God in my soul. Before I could marry her son, she insisted I attend the Baptist Church in Goose Creek, South Carolina, where she was a member, and be saved. Mrs. Simpson was a wonderful, loving woman to me, and, I believe, she endured the same kinds of hardships my mother had endured with an abusive husband. The difference was that Mrs. Simpson walked with the Lord God and was in His Word, the Bible, constantly. She had a sense of peace even when she was surrounded by chaos. She even had an angelic glow around her, which I have only observed around two women in my life. Even though that Sunday in May of 1972 I came forward in the church to make a commitment to God and agreed to a baptism by submersion in water,

I would backslide often. My dear Mrs. Simpson passed in 2013 after a lengthy struggle with dementia. The following passage from Matthew really spoke to me after her passing: "Come to me, all you who are weary and burdened, and I will give you rest. Take my yoke upon you and learn from me, for I am gentle and humble in heart, and you will find rest for your souls. For my yoke is easy and my burden is light" (Matt. 11:28-30).

It took me many years, trials, and tribulations before I learned to give up to the Lord Jesus my burdens, pray for His wisdom and guidance, and then let go and let Him lead me.

Deborah's mother, Momma,
Canon, Georgia, 1952

The Journey Across America

In Charleston, South Carolina, during the summer of 1972, someone called my mother and told her I was pregnant. I had been in denial and hadn't had a menstrual period in two months. I was so confused about what to do and who to talk to. Obviously one of my girlfriends, or one of their mothers, made that decision for me. Momma did need to know. Even though I was scared to death of her reaction, and ashamed, I was relieved that someone squealed on me. That day Momma took me to the hospital for a pregnancy test. The test confirmed what she and I already knew. Her oldest daughter was pregnant. That same evening, Momma told my Navy Petty Officer father the news.

In my junior year of high school, I had met David Simpson. He was so handsome, kind, and considerate. He was a senior, was six feet, four inches tall, was 190 pounds of muscle, was a high school football player, drove a beautiful powder blue sports car, and had thick, silky, blond hair and beautiful blue eyes. He was a gorgeous hunk of a man. All the girls were chasing after him, but he turned his attention toward me one day after the football game. I was so thrilled and would do anything to make him happy and keep him with me. Whatever it took! Besides, within a couple of months of dating, we were engaged. Or, at least, that's what he said. I was easily persuaded. I was sixteen, had raging hormones, and was desperate to leave the abusive environment at home. Just maybe he would be my way out?

When my father found out I was pregnant, he paid a visit to David's father. They agreed his son and I should be married soon. Two months later, we were married in that same little Baptist Church in which his mother had me come forward and accept the Lord and get baptized.

A couple of weeks later, David and I attended our first parenting and birthing class at the Charleston Navy Hospital. The hospital must have been built during the Civil War right after Fort Sumter. It was a massive brick structure, lacking character, warmth, or organization, and I'm sure it was haunted. David and I sat on floor mats with the other couples. We were wide-eyed, shocked, and speechless as the movie we viewed showed a basketball-sized baby coming out of a woman! We never went back to the birthing classes and decided it was best not to think about that part of the process. Instead, we enjoyed warm, loving moments together as the baby grew and kicked in my belly.

Within two months, David was shipped off to Army basic training at Fort Jackson in Columbia, SC. After basic training, he was shipped to Fort Dix, New Jersey, back home to Charleston for Christmas, and then assigned to Fort Wainwright, Alaska. While David was home for Christmas, on December 23, 1972, a brutally cold night at the old haunted Civil War Naval Hospital in downtown Charleston, Frances Lynne Simpson was born. It was a horrible experience, and I screamed bloody murder the whole time! We named Frances after my mother. Of course, Daddy took one look at baby Frances and announced to David, "I don't think that's your baby. Look at that thick head of black hair and black eyes!" Thanks, Dad, for instilling suspicion in a jealous young husband! Of course, it was his baby, but the stage had been set for doubt. David was off to Alaska two days later. Baby Frances and I would join him January 3, 1973, in Fairbanks, Alaska.

In December 1972, when Frances was born, the hospital did not promote breastfeeding. They gave me a shot to dry up my breast milk. Baby formula, they said, was much more nourishing, portable, and better for the babies. At least that's what the nurse said when they sent me home the next day with three cans of sample formula and a coupon for more.

Frances was ten days old when we left Charleston for Fairbanks, Alaska, and the Fort Wainwright Army base. At seventeen years of age, I had never been on an airplane, so it was very exciting! When we had traveled to Illinois, California, Virginia, Georgia, and South Carolina to join Daddy when I was a young girl, we had always driven. In fact, I had been the navigator and had read the maps to Momma.

I was not worried about traveling with baby Frances. She slept most of the time, and I had the formula premeasured in baby bottles in the diaper bag. I felt like I could handle this maternal activity with ease and felt very confident. Before the end of the day, I would realize what a horrible mom and idiot I was! Thank goodness social media had not been invented yet. I would have been all over the Internet, Headline News for sure: "Charleston Miracle - Southern redneck makes it all the way to Alaska!"

The Charleston weather that day was cool with a misty rain, maybe forty degrees. At the airport, I had Frances all bundled up in her new baby carrier. Momma noticed she looked strange in the carrier, and when I checked on Frances, she was upside down with her head hanging downward and her feet up in the air! My maternal difficulties didn't stop there, though. Later, at security, the personnel asked that all items be placed on the conveyer belt for X-ray. I placed the coats, diaper bag, purse, and baby in the carrier on the conveyor and walked through the detector. Much to my surprise, there was such a commotion behind me. When I turned around, they were screaming to shut down the conveyer. Some idiot had put a baby in the machine! By now you know who that was!

The flights took more than sixteen hours from Charleston to Fairbanks. By the time I got on the Alaskan Airlines flight out of Seattle, the baby formula was spoiled.

I had premeasured and poured the mixture in bottles before we left. Now they were just spoiled, smelly blobs in the baby bottles. Baby Frances was awake, hungry, and crying. I asked the flight attendant for help. Any milk, cream? Anything that I could feed this ten-day-old baby? Nothing, she said. Not even creamers for coffee. Based on the condescending look I got from her, she obviously thought I was an idiot who should not be allowed to have children. So, Frances cried, and I started crying too because I was such a stupid mom. I didn't know that formula spoiled, and I felt like such a horrible mother.

Next to me on the plane was a burly Alaskan Eskimo with a beautiful, round face. He was a big, dark-skinned man, with rough, sunbaked hands and a face with a smile that could light up a room. His eyes sparkled, and his hands were the size of a basketball. He had on the full hooded parka and looked like he would be leading a sled dog team when he got to Fairbanks. He looked at me, looked at Frances, and asked if he could hold her. I could hear my mother's voice saying, "No, no, no! Don't let anyone touch your baby!" But, desperate, with tears running down both cheeks, I handed her over. Looking back, I believe he was an angel from Heaven. This sweet, gentle, sunbaked, burly man laid Frances's tiny body on his furry parka and sang softly for the two-hour flight. She barely moved and went soundly to sleep. To this day, I think that man was the embodiment of the Psalm: "The LORD is gracious and righteous; our God is full of compassion. The LORD protects the unwary; when I was brought low, he saved me" (Ps. 116:5–6).

When we got off the plane in Fairbanks, it was seventy-two degrees below zero. I could hardly breathe; it was so cold, my lungs hurt. My mother was convinced that we would be living in an igloo and that neither Frances nor I would survive this tour of duty. She wasn't far from the truth. The ice fog that day in Fairbanks could be cut with a knife, and the visibility was just a few feet. Even though it was the middle of the day, the sky was black. In January, you have almost twenty-four hours of darkness in Fairbanks. Due to the severe cold and darkness, Frances and I spent almost all our time in the little white cabin David rented outside the base. We were waiting on base housing to be available, and there was a backlog.

The little white house with two rooms and a cellar was haunted. Or did I have cabin fever? Whatever it was, it was real, and I feared for my life and the life of baby Frances every moment in that house. Every day, it was bitter cold. Every day, David unplugged the car block heater and would go to work at the base in the only car we shared. And every day, the picture of Jesus hanging on the kitchen wall would follow me with His eyes no matter where I went in the house. I could feel His eyes on me even in the bedroom or bathroom. The banging sounds coming from the cellar below the kitchen were deafening. David told me he did not hear a thing. *Liar! He must be trying to drive me crazy*, I thought. To keep the monster in the cellar, I pulled the kitchen table over the trap door. I would watch the door for movement while Jesus watched me from His picture above the trap door in the kitchen.

With no TV and very few books to read, I thank God I had Frances to take care of. She needed me! Otherwise, I do believe I would have lost my mind. At least, what was left of it. Summer finally came, along with its twenty-four hours of daylight. Life was so much better, and most importantly, we moved into base housing.

In the summer, Alaska is God's country—full of light, animals, flowers, and cheer. Everyone seems to have a positive attitude. On the way to summer in the spring, and in the fall season, you'll see the northern lights in the sky. Like waves, they dance in unison with blue, red, yellow, and green colors. One time, driving home from the grocery store, I had to pull over for ten minutes and just admire the amazing display of color and dancing brilliance in the northern sky. My jaw dropped to the ground at the sight, and I was thinking, "Momma, you sure don't see this in Charleston." It was surely a "Wow" moment. Of course, I did not have a camera in the car to record the atmospheric phenomenon.

To the north of Fairbanks were the Arctic Circle, the Yukon River, and the tundra. In the summer, the tundra was full of brilliant flowers in red, blue, and yellow for as far as the eye could see. Bears, moose, various birds, and arctic hares roamed the tundra and were a sight to see. Headed south of Fairbanks, we would come to the Denali National Park, the Alaska Range, and Mount McKinley, the highest peak in North America. In this area, you could observe bears (black and grizzly), moose, hares, wolves, and caribou, at a minimum. We saw Dall sheep strategically balanced on many of the mountainous outcroppings. There were also miles of beautiful tundra to observe in the Denali National Park, and the tundra was full of life. David and I loved Alaska in the summer, but it was a pit in the winter—dark, cold, forbidden—and the demons came out of the dark and possessed the people. Drinking, divorce, and suicide were rampant. It was like the Devil took control when the darkness covered the land.

As a family, David, Frances, and I left Fairbanks eighteen months after our arrival and headed for a new assignment at Fort Gordon, Georgia, near Augusta. My relationship with David had deteriorated greatly during our time in Fairbanks. I knew he had a series of mistresses he would visit in Fairbanks, and we argued about him spending grocery money on beer and other women. The arguments did not stop his overnight stays.

When we loaded the car to head south to Augusta, Georgia, I was four months pregnant with Melanie, my second daughter. I could only hope that David's and my relationship would somehow improve once he was away from his Alaskan drinking buddies and mistresses. Plus, in Augusta, I would be closer to my Momma and Dad in Charleston. I guess I was seeking a sense of security and hoped I could spend more time with my mother and little sister.

The 1600-mile trip down the Alaska Highway through Canada was beautiful even though the road was gravel and dirt. The animals, mountains, plants, and valleys were breathtaking in the summer of 1974. There were no guardrails to keep you from sliding off the side of the cliff, but their absence also permitted the most beautiful, unobstructed view of the wilderness. We might go a full day before seeing a gas station or a small hotel. It might be two hours before we saw another vehicle on the highway. It was desolate, and I knew we had to be prepared to take care of ourselves if anything happened. There were no rest stops for water, no hospitals, and no auto parts stores.

About one hundred miles into Canada, David stopped the red Ford mustang when he spotted a black bear cub about fifty feet from the road. I said, "Are you nuts?! Momma bear is nearby!" I sat in the car counting in my mind the insurance money and watching this idiot chase a small bear around the hillside in a desolate part of Canada. Momma bear must have been busy because she spared David that day. Not long after his bear cub chase, we passed an eighteen-wheeler, and a piece of gravel hit and split the front windshield.

When we had left Fairbanks three days earlier, the weather was warm, dry, and in the fifties. In fact, the truckdrivers at the diner that morning had said they were racing to get so many trucks across the Yukon River before it broke up. Due to the Alaskan pipeline, a bridge was now needed across the Yukon. Since the weather had been so nice, I had worn flipflops, my favorite footwear, and loose summer clothes. David had put on a pair of tennis shoes with his lightweight clothing. Through Canada, the temperatures were mild, and the sky was sunny the whole time—just spectacular views through the Canadian Rockies. Unfortunately, my camera battery died the first day on the road, so I did not get even one picture.

Our luck really ran out in North Dakota, though. In the distance south of Edmonton, Canada, we could see the dark clouds forming. We did not realize we were headed into a severe snowstorm in North Dakota. Once we went through US customs at the border, it hit us full blast with winds of sixty to eighty miles an hour and temperatures dropping into the twenties and thirties. On the Interstate, numerous trucks and cars were overturned in the median. Other than stopping for gas, we inched our way through the storm for twelve hours until we collapsed in the cheap hotel bed. I was so embarrassed by my flipflops when we stopped but hated to spend money on something I did not need even more. All our shoes had been shipped with the furniture on to Augusta.

In Fort Gordon, many of the neighbors in our trailer park were Army troops with their wives and children. We were just over a mile from the front gate of the base, and for some reason we did not attempt to secure military housing in Augusta. Maybe there was a shortage? Two doors down were Dan and his wife, Kathy, both nurses. Dan was maybe five feet, six inches tall like me and was light skinned with short, light brown hair, a little chubby with a mustache. He was plain looking, and the same was true for his wife, Kathy. They did not possess any striking characteristics or mannerisms. She was slim, with brown, shoulder length hair and brown eyes, maybe five feet, five inches tall. Both were outgoing and easy friends. By then, I was eight months pregnant with our second child.

One evening, Dan and Kathy came over and decided we should be dancing in the trailer living room to some top forty hits on the radio. Everyone but me had been drinking and smoking weed. Dan turned on the radio and asked to dance with me. I said no, but he insisted. He pulled me close and put his hands on my big belly, rubbing gently. I was terrified and pushed him away. Dan apologized, saying how much he loved pregnant women and how he wished he and Kathy could have had children. David told me that night that Dan and Kathy had an unusual "open" marriage arrangement. *Great*, I thought, *weirdos two doors down!* From that point forward, I just considered Dan strange and never let him or his wife in the house unless David was present. I was cold and distant to them both. Dan tried to visit a couple of times when David was not home. Through the trailer door, I told him to go away.

Like our home in Fairbanks, the two-bedroom trailer near Fort Gordon in Augusta, Georgia, was haunted too. In bed at night while David was on night shift, I kept the gun handy under the edge of the bed and would listen to what I thought was someone breathing. My second daughter, Melanie, was born a month premature and slept peacefully in the basinet next to the bed. It was not her soft, quiet breathing I heard. It was a deep-throated sound, and sometimes it sounded like a man snoring. I followed the sound several times, and it always led me to the refrigerator, which was on the wall right behind the bed headboard. I even pulled the refrigerator out one night into the middle of the kitchen floor, trying to find the source of the strange sound. This went on for weeks and seemed to be prevalent on the nights that David had night shift at the base. One night, when David was home unexpectedly, I heard the breathing. I had told David about the sounds several times, but it never occurred when he was home. That night was the exception. I gently woke him up and asked him to listen. After a few minutes, he clearly heard the breathing I was hearing. He got up quietly and went into the kitchen. I put Melanie in the bed with me. Frances was sound asleep in her bed at the other end of the trailer. I had just checked on her, as I did often at night.

David traced the sound to the refrigerator also. When he did not find anything behind the refrigerator, with a flashlight and the 32-caliber handgun in hand, he went out the small trailer door off the kitchen to look under the house. As the door opened, the breathing stopped, and I heard a shuffle under the trailer and screaming. It was Dan! I don't know why David did not shoot him! He held the gun on Dan while he made excuses. He said he had been chasing an animal under our trailer that night. David let Dan go, but he investigated the area under the trailer. He found some of my clothes, stolen from the clothesline, on the ground where Dan had been sleeping, obviously on a regular basis. Dan was a full-blown pervert!

The next morning, David went to his Supervisor and Commanding Officer at Fort Gordon about Dan's behavior. Within two days, the military nurses, Dan and Kathy, were gone. I heard they were shipped to Germany.

The Trip Back Home to Charleston

We spent twelve months at Fort Gordon, Georgia, and then we were transferred to Fort Huachuca, Arizona, south of Tucson in Sierra Vista. The town of Sierra Vista is considered a high desert at 4600 feet above sea level. David's and my marriage was still deteriorating, but now I had two babies to feed and had very little education, no work experience, and no money of my own. I could not bring myself to call and go home to Momma and Daddy. I knew what Momma had put up with, and my circumstances just did not seem that bad...yet.

Before moving on base at Fort Huachuca, on the outskirts of the town Sierra Vista, we lived in a small, two-bedroom apartment. Several one-story apartments were on each side of a concrete path maybe ten feet wide. Parking was in the back. Sierra Vista is a desert town located about fifteen miles north of the Mexican border and the town of Nogales. I had never seen such desert vegetation, cacti, or strange critters. The coarse, sandy soil lacked any moisture, and it would not rain for months. When it did rain, the desert flowers would bloom like it was their only chance to shine, even just for a day or two. That first winter in Fort Huachuca, it snowed in the desert! It was a freak storm and just a dusting of snow that lasted maybe two hours. But it was a gorgeous sight to behold. All those beautiful saguaro and agaves cacti covered with snow. I knew the tarantulas would be snuggled up together in their desert burrow-homes.

Each Saturday we organized a desert tarantula spider race. In the beginning, the girls and I were scared to death of the big spiders. But once we had our very own tarantula in the race, we were cheering him on with long sticks to guide him along the race route. There was a small pool of money to be won, and God knows we needed it. I found out right away that David was still openly selling weed in Arizona. I was so upset! I did not trust the people he brought to the apartment. They knew he had drugs and cash stashed away. I knew I had to protect my children. I was beginning to realize that the girls and I could be in grave danger. I wondered if Frances, Melanie, and I were just a front to hide his drug selling activities. He did not seem to care one way or the other about us. David was arrested at one point and worked something out with the local police and the base Commanding Officer. He did not go to jail. Drugs like marijuana were illegal but very prevalent in the Army at that time.

After about three months, we moved from the apartment into Fort Huachuca base housing. I applied and started working at the Officers Club on base as a waitress. The base Child Care Center was along the route to the Officers Club. I had found a plastic bike seat where both girls could ride with me, stacked behind me on the bicycle. I would drop them off at the center and pick them up coming home from work. The people I worked with were kind, considerate, and respectful, and I was truly happy and enjoying myself for the first time in a long time. My supervisor, an older German waitress, took me under her wing, and I thank God for her support, guidance, and kindness. She was the only one I shared my family situation with. The tips from the waitress work more than covered the child care cost, and I had money left to consider college. When I got married at seventeen, I had promised my father I would finish high school, and I did—in Alaska. I got a General Education Diploma (GED) as promised. Now I wanted to continue my education and enroll at the local community college. David was not pleased with my new-found confidence and independence and made his feelings known.

I worked hard, enjoyed the waitress job, and took care of my girls. I felt a bit of self-confidence for the first time in years. I prayed for guidance, and everything seemed so much more joyful. My real priorities seemed to be coming into focus.

One morning it was raining hard, and I was scheduled to work the lunch shift, so I asked David if I could take the car instead of the bike. He said no. He had worked the night before and had, to my knowledge, no commitments that day. He was just being selfish, mean, and trying to make me late. I was mad and slammed the bedroom door behind me. As I walked down the hall to the kitchen where the girls were having cereal, he came out of the room like a giant angry bear I had woken from hibernation. With his six-foot, four-inch frame and 200 pounds of muscle, he grabbed me from the back by my long hair and tossed my body against the washer and dryer. My five-foot, five-inch frame and 105-pound body hit the machine hard, and I knew I was hurt. I could hardly breathe, and the girls were crying and screaming. I somehow managed to tell David I would rather die than stay with him. He must have realized at that point that his hold on me had been broken, and he left the house. For years he had been telling me if I left him, he would take the girls and kill me. I missed work that day, and I finally called Momma and Daddy for help. I told them what had been going on for years. I cried, they cried, and we put together a plan for me to leave.

In church that Sunday in Sierra Vista, Arizona, I listened intently to the pastor's message, and I asked the Lord God to help me. At that moment, when I finished the sincerest prayer I had ever spoken, a tremendous weight lifted off my shoulders. I knew from that moment on everything would be fine. I knew it was God's will for the girls and me to be happy and that it was OK for David not to be part of our future. I clung to the Bible verse that says, "For the eyes of the Lord are on the righteous and his ears are attentive to their prayer, but the face of the Lord is against those who do evil" (1 Pet. 3:12).

With Momma and Daddy's help, I moved out of the base housing and into a small second floor apartment just outside the base gate in Sierra Vista. David did not come around to bother me or to see his daughters. I think he was glad to finally get rid of us. I added a second job to my schedule in town and asked David for the old 1972 Chevrolet Kingswood four-door station wagon he had bought from his friend who was going overseas. Two months later in Tombstone, Arizona, I was divorced, and the station wagon, the girls, and fifty dollars per month of child support from David were mine in the settlement. David only paid one month of child support, and that was only because I called his Commanding Officer, and he was forced to pay. I never saw a penny again, court order or not.

Momma sent me her VISA credit card with a letter giving me permission to use it to pay for the U-Haul, gas, and hotels. She sent maps from AAA that detailed the 2000-mile route from Sierra Vista, Arizona, to Charleston, South Carolina, for the girls and me. Mommas think of everything! The old Kingswood wagon had a serious oil leak, bald tires, and an expired tag. The German waitress at the Officers Club gave me her old tires when she upgraded and even paid to have them mounted and balanced on my car. She said mine were not safe. I think she got those new tires on her car just to help me. She was a wonderful woman, my supervisor, and a true blessing from God. I wish I had stayed in touch with her and could have somehow paid her back. But I have faith in God's Word, which states, "Give, and it will be given to you. A good measure, pressed down, shaken together and running over, will be poured into your lap. For with the measure you use, it will be measured to you" (Lk. 6:38). I have no doubt that God will pay her back for me because He said He would in this Scripture.

When I went to the tag office to get a new license plate for the station wagon, I found out that David had not had his friend sign over the car title properly. The new plate was now out of the question since the guy was stationed overseas, and I was leaving for Charleston in a couple of days. My Alaska driver's license had recently expired too, so I went to the Motor Vehicle office to get a new one. *At least I can be a legal driver*, I thought. The Motor Vehicle office said they would need to wait for my records from Alaska before they would give me an Arizona license. Back then everything went by postal mail. So, I packed the U-Haul trailer, put the girls in the wagon, and I headed north on Highway 90 out of Sierra Vista, Arizona, with no car tag, no valid driver's license, no car insurance, and the back window taped over where the glass was busted out—and a prayer. The U-Haul trailer fortunately had a valid tag, and I'm sure that kept me from being pulled over.

We were on our way with a prayer from friends, Momma's VISA, and a sense of freedom I had not felt since I was seventeen. I just focused then on getting us home safely to Charleston. Nothing beyond that was important at that moment. I was twenty-one years old. Frances was three years old and Melanie one year old.

In the wagon, I had put the back seats down, so the girls had a nice seating and play area, making maybe a five-by-four-foot carpeted area. This was their eating, playing, and sleeping area for four days on the road. The goldfish, goldfish bowl, and barrel cactus were in the front seat with me. Strapped on the top of the car was the bike with the plastic child carrier attached. The bike had come to represent the instrument of independence from the angry bear man. Just a few miles down the road, the tire from the bike on the roof came through the taped-up back window and stayed there for the duration of the trip.

I had never driven a car pulling a six-by-ten-foot trailer behind it. The car and the trailer were loaded, and the Kingswood station wagon was straining. Black smoke poured out of the back of the wagon, and the cars passing us on the two-lane highway out of Sierra Vista were honking continually.

The first night we made it to downtown El Paso, Texas. It was one o'clock in the morning, and I was exhausted. A neon sign on Interstate 10 announced a Holiday Inn at the next exit. Momma had recommended staying at the Holiday Inn, and I trusted Momma. I maneuvered the caravan into the drive leading up to the entrance and staggered into the lobby like a drunk.

Frances and I had food stains on our clothes and must have looked like some hillbillies from the west. Melanie had pooped in her diaper and was stinky. The hotel attendant processed the credit card and handed me a key. Then I asked her where the parking lot was. She said, "Pull forward about fifty yards, turn right, and you are in the parking lot." *Cool!* I thought. *I must have missed it in the dark.* We pulled forward, turned right, and the sign said that if you were pulling "anything" to go to the fourth floor. The U-Haul trailer scraped on each floor, but I kept going to the fourth floor of the parking lot and made it! I took my nasty, stinky self and children, plus one small bag, and boarded the elevator.

On the elevator were two good looking couples who had obviously been enjoying a night on the town. They gave me a nasty look and huddled in the elevator corner, exiting on the next floor.

When we got to the fourteenth floor, I cleaned up the girls and everyone climbed into bed. I called Momma on the hotel phone to give her an update. I asked God to protect and guide the girls and me. Melanie and Frances were sound asleep when their heads hit the pillow. But I could not sleep. I was scared to death that we would have a fire during the night, and I could not figure out how to tie enough sheets, clothes, and pillowcases together to rescue the girls and me. I had never stayed above the second floor in a hotel, and none of my travel hotels with David had been as nice as this Holiday Inn. In hindsight, I should have located the fire escape stairs, devised a plan, and slept like a baby.

The next day, with help from an El Paso policeman, who, for whatever reason, happened to be in the garage that morning, we took the U-Haul back down the indoor garage ramps. I swore we would never stay at a high-rise hotel with indoor parking ever again. To this day, I thank God that the El Paso police officer decided to overlook my missing car tag.

In the car, the girls had learned that I could swing my arm behind me just so far to smack them if they got out of line. And they were getting out of line often! It was my way of breaking up fights, arguments, and roughhousing in the seat behind me. Of course, at that time, seatbelts and a child seat were not required. They had a certain amount of mobility to move around the car. By that point, I had learned that each time an eighteen-wheeler roared pass me on I-10 at seventy miles an hour, the trailer and car would shake, rock, and roll. It was so scary! It was important that I keep both hands on the wheel and control the vehicle when this happened, especially since it was pouring down rain. Well, just as I noticed a new eighteen-wheeler approaching, I heard the window rolling down behind me. I said, "Girls!! Get away from that window—get away from that door!" Meanwhile, they continued to roll the window down. They knew I was busy holding the wheel and that my arm could not reach them when they were directly behind my seat. I felt the truck wheels pass and heard both girls scream over the pounding rain. I looked back, and both girls were covered with mud. Served them right for not listening! The goldfish and I had a good laugh.

Melanie kept crawling up to the back of the front seat and throwing stuff in the goldfish bowl. He had candy, a toothbrush, and one pink sock to keep him company.

It was a long day, fourteen hours of driving, but the second night we made it to west Louisiana. I was determined to get out of Texas. The Holiday Inn was a two-story structure adjacent to the interstate with parking next to the room. Thank you, Jesus! I asked for the first floor and we got a key. Our room was an internal room looking out on the pool in the middle of the building's square layout. When we got to the room, the key would not fit. I set the girls and the suitcase by the room door and said, "DO NOT MOVE." I ran, I mean RAN, back to the lobby, fully aware of the pool with no occupants and my girls, who could not swim, back by the room door. I opened the lobby door, slipped on the threshold, and skidded into the lobby on my belly. After they helped me up off the floor, I babbled something about needing a key, they handed me a new key, and I ran back as fast as I could. Both girls were sitting by the door and had not moved an inch. Before I went to sleep, I called Momma.

On the road the third day, between Louisiana and Georgia, we had more rain and many detours. The detours through Alabama were narrow, two-lane roads, and the semi-trucks seemed to take both lanes, coming and going. At one point I met a large semi on a narrow bridge with my U-Haul trailer in tow. It had to have been the hand of God who reached down and kept the two large vehicles separated on that narrow bridge. In Alabama, we stopped at a small roadside restaurant on the detour route. It was still pouring, but my nerves were shot. We washed up, ate like little piglets, changed Melanie's diaper, and got back on the road. Maneuvering out of the small, crowded parking lot, I hit another car. I looked at the other vehicle through my rearview mirror and the heavy rain. It did not appear to have a dent. With no car tag, no license, and no insurance, I kept on going. God, forgive me, please.

The third day we made it to central Georgia. Beginning that day, every time I filled the gas tank, I would add a quart of oil. The smoke cloud following the car was getting worse and worse, and the tree-lined hills of Alabama and Georgia did not help one bit. I was flying down the road on recapped tires and a prayer! Every mile marker we flew past was a blessing and brought us one mile closer to Charleston. I did not have a back-up plan in case the car broke down. I knew it was God's will that I make it to Charleston.

At a gas station in Georgia, a strange, scruffy-looking man approached the car as I was filling up. A feeling of true danger and dread came over me. I looked in the car and said, "Honey wake up! I think someone is here to see you." The man did an about face and left. Strange...

That night at the Georgia Holiday Inn, we had to go to the second floor, and when I opened the door, someone was in the room. Oh my gosh! At least that time, as we worked our way back to the lobby, the attendant came running with a new key and escorted the girls and me to a new room...which lacked power, so we moved again.

Late on the fourth day since leaving Sierra Vista, Arizona, we finally arrived at Momma's in Charleston, South Carolina. She saw us pull up and came running out with my little sister, Cindy. I will always remember very vividly the tears in Momma's eyes and her comment, "I can't believe you made it!" But we did—I knew we would—and it was only by the grace of God. His arms were around the girls and me the whole time. I knew it in my heart and soul. Scripture says, "Answer me when I call to you, my righteous God. Give me relief from my distress; have mercy on me and hear my prayer. In peace I will lie down and sleep, for you alone, LORD, make me dwell in safety" (Ps. 4:1, 8). I felt God's mercy on us that whole trip.

That night, I slept like a baby. Also that night, the temperature dipped below freezing in Charleston. With all the excitement of the arrival, I had left the goldfish and the barrel cactus in the car. They froze. The goldfish bowl still had Melanie's toothbrush sticking out of the frozen sheet of ice.

Deborah, Frances, and Melanie, Charleston, South Carolina, 1976

Working in a Male-Dominated Industry

*N*ot long after getting back to Charleston, my father, who was contracting in Mobile, Alabama, asked me to join him and help get his Quality Inspection crew "straightened out." It was a fantastic opportunity to use my administrative, planning, and organizational skills. I agreed to take the job, and the girls and I moved to Alabama. We established quality control practices and procedures for the team. Daddy was the Project Manager and Level III Inspector over six technicians performing ultrasonic, radiograph, and liquid penetrant inspections. We worked under the direction of the Corp of Engineers, testing and inspecting the tanks being built for liquified natural gas (LNG) transport, both domestic and internationally. Each tank held 85 million gallons of LNG, and the tank weldments required 100 percent ultrasonic inspection.

I helped Daddy set up the program and then took on the inspection duties as a helper—Level I Technician. I worked my way up through the training and inspection performance activities to Level II in all areas very quickly. The worst part was the porta-potties everyone had to use. They were full of crabs.

The girls and I loved the Mobile area, which was near the Gulf Shores National Seashore. Weekends at the white sandy beach with work friends were great fun.

When the contract ended in Mobile at the end of 1977, the girls and I went back to Charleston. Briefly I worked as a cocktail waitress at the local Sheraton. Every weekend this Sheraton had a great band and was packed with customers. I looked like a penguin in my uniform: white, fitted shirt; black bathing suit bottom with tights; and black, high-heeled shoes. The penguin, long-tail, fitted cape was worn like a jacket over the outfit. Momma would not let me leave the house in it. She insisted I cover it up so the neighbors could not see what I was wearing. I thought the outfit was cute and very attractive on me. She said it looked trashy. Regardless, along with a minimal pay check, I got at least one hundred dollars in tips each Friday and Saturday night. In 1977 and early 1978, that was good money.

After working a brief period in the service industry, I noticed an ad in the local Charleston paper. The utility, Southern Carolina Electric and Gas (SCE&G) was approved by the Nuclear Regulator and the Public Service Commission in South Carolina to build a nuclear power plant. I was thrilled when I applied and was interviewed and they asked me to join the SCE&G team as their Quality Control (QC) Inspector, Mechanical, starting in March 1978. My experience in Mobile, Alabama, had opened the door for this opportunity. But they were also looking to satisfy their affirmative action commitments and needed a few good women in this male-dominated discipline at the power plant. You see, the US government had determined that women were not getting the opportunities that men were and set quotas for companies to follow. I didn't know what the quotas or milestone objective totals were for SCE&G, but I was honored to be part of the experiment and make enough money to support my family. The experience and ultrasonic inspection certifications I had achieved in Mobile on the LNG tank inspection activities qualified me for this position as a Level I QC Inspector in training. By the time I left the power plant two years later, I was a qualified and certified QC Inspector, Level II, for Mechanical, Electrical, Instrument & Control (I&C), Visual and Welding.

Life was good except for the male chauvinist attitudes at the plant. The Mechanical QC Inspectors for SCE&G plant construction totaled six including the supervisor. John was the supervisor, and the others were Ricky, Cary, Tim, James, and me. I never really felt welcome but instead was tolerated. They called me the "token female" since everyone knew the company had to satisfy affirmative action goals. I just worked harder, studied more, and tried to fit in. It was especially hard at lunch time because the Mechanical QC construction trailer the six of us worked out of was covered wall to wall with girlie pictures. No matter where you sat, you were looking at some part of a woman. I think the guys liked seeing me cringe at all of those pictures in my face anytime I was in the trailer. Of course, I minimized that time and stayed on the plant floor except for lunch. I finally had the nerve after six months to tell John I wanted to bring in my own picture for the trailer section assigned to me and where I sat for lunch. He just laughed and didn't say anything else, so I bought my first *Playgirl* magazine. At that time, it had a foldout picture of a very handsome young man, which I displayed in front of my seat. Of course, in hindsight, I was just lowering my standards to theirs. I should have known better.

After I posted the picture of the man, the crap really hit the fan! Ricky and Cary came in and both said, "Take it down. Take it down now!"

John, the supervisor, was not there, but I held my ground and said, "No." I said, "If you can have all those women plastered all over the trailer, I can have my man!"

That's when Cary took out a knife and said if I did not take it down, he would stab me.

Oh man! What do I do now? I was thinking.

Two more QC inspectors showed up and told Cary to put the knife away. He was furious, and the look in his eyes was scary. If no one else had been there, I am sure he would have stabbed me. The others saw this and could tell I was in real danger. They moved in between Cary and me, then, threatening to take the knife from him and begging him to put it down, and that's when John, the supervisor, came through the door. Cary stormed out of the trailer door with the others right behind him. John considered what had just happened and proceeded to take down ALL the pictures. Tore them off the wall. Including mine.

Now ALL the guys were mad at me. They never spoke to me again unless they had to. Shortly thereafter, I found a place in the turbine building with the Welding Superintendent, Freddie, to have lunch. He had a spare Gang Box, and it was my new office and lunch area. No nasty pictures to look at either. Freddie wouldn't put up with that. He was twice my age and a father figure. I was performing Welding Inspection by then on the turbine secondary side of the plant. So I just told John, my supervisor, that the new work office was closer to my work area. He understood and agreed it was a better arrangement for me.

Not long after that, the QC Inspectors who were so mad at me invited me to a party. I thought maybe they were feeling bad about how they had treated me and wanted to make amends. Plus, I thought I might meet some of their wives who I had heard so much about. I did not get out much with the long hours and having two young children, so I was looking forward to the get together. When I got there, the women were absent. The men were drinking and watching football. They insisted I have a beer, even though I did not drink at the time. I thought surely one would be fine, and they had munchies to snack on. Suddenly, I had a horrible headache. I never had headaches. I asked Ricky if he had an aspirin or something for a headache. He did, and he gave it to me with a clear liquid I thought was water. Shortly thereafter, I told the guys I did not feel that great and was going home. I said my goodbyes and staggered to the car. I felt so dizzy and sick. In the car, I realized I was seeing double of everything. I did not know how, but I knew I had to get home to the girls and the babysitter.

Looking back, the guys were probably watching from the window and laughing at me, like, "Look at her! Can't even take one beer!" Fortunately, the party location was about a mile from my apartment. I covered one eye and managed to get back home. God even protects idiots! It had to be by the grace of God again because I don't remember anything more after starting the drive home.

The next morning, I woke up alone in my own bed, my girls were fine, and the babysitter was home safe. Years later, when I look back, I believe those men either put something in the beer to drug me, and it gave me the horrible headache, and/or they gave me vodka or some sort of drug to swallow the aspirin. Those coworkers were satanic evil men, determined to destroy me. I was far too trusting. Finally, I saw clearly what was happening and their true venomous hate for me. This was the one and only time in my life that I was in such a drugged state of mind and seeing double of everything. From then on, I kept my distance from the QC Inspectors. It was probably two years before I drank any alcohol again, and it was a long time before I trusted any man at a party or bar again.

In early 1980, after power plant system hot functional testing, construction of the power plant was complete. I was laid off, along with a majority of the 800 plus employees working at that time. Frances, Melanie, and I loaded the U-Haul and headed back to Momma's in Charleston.

Florida QC Inspector and Jerry

Shortly after my layoff from SCE&G, the Plant Manager for a Florida Nuclear Power Plant was interviewing in Charleston for Instrument & Control (I&C) Technicians. I believe from the moment he met me that he had me pegged as his new Quality Control (QC) Inspector. He flew me down to Florida for an interview with the immediate supervisor and allowed an extra day so that I could check out the Crystal River area, just north of Tampa. The Crystal River population was around 5,000 people. In the spring of 1980, the city, the springs, and Crystal Bay in the Crystal River were pristine! I had never seen such beautiful, clear streams, lakes, and waterways. The fish—mullet, trout, and bream—and sea cows, which they called manatees, were swimming under my rental canoe, and I could see everything through the eight feet of water as clear as day! I knew the girls would love this place. Plus, the power plant was ten minutes from town. In South Carolina, I had driven forty-five minutes to and from work, which took a lot of time out of the day just for travel.

When I started work, the other inspectors, George, Jim, and Mike, seemed supportive. And why wouldn't they be? Before I showed up, they were on call for evening and weekend inspections every third week. Now they could move to every fourth week. They were thrilled that I could hit the ground running as a certified QC Inspector based on my experience in South Carolina. I suppose I didn't get the best first impression of George when he told me the first week that I was "taking a man's job." I told him I needed to support my family just like he did, and after an awkward silence, he walked away. Of all the inspectors, George was the most meticulous. He was tall and thin with light-colored hair and blue eyes and was maybe twenty-five years old like me. His attention to detail was above reproach, and he annoyed the heck out of me. My inspection reports were a one-page factual summary. His were books like the novel *War and Peace*! But I told others who would get impatient with George that if I ever needed someone to inspect my vehicle or safety gear before use, I wanted George.

The Crystal River Nuclear Power Plant went on line, or began operations, in 1979. When I came along in the spring of 1980, because the plant was operational, I had to go through radiation training. Health Physics

(HP) personnel gave me a small, black, rectangular pin, maybe one-half inch by one inch, to clip to my clothes and a small, six-inch long, round tube, maybe one-half inch in diameter, called a dosimeter. Both instruments monitored my radiation exposure. The HP technician showed me the dress out process and dress out room, then turned me loose to inspect equipment in the radiation-controlled areas of the plant. Not all areas of the plant were radiated. For example, on the secondary side were the steam turbine, condenser, moisture separators, and much more, which were not radiated, and I could simply wear my street clothes and hard hat. However, if the system of pipes, pumps, and valves met the radiated fuel or fuel byproducts, it was irradiated, and you had to be monitored for exposure.

The clothing overgarments usually consisted of white overalls, booties over your shoes, and two sets of gloves. The first set of gloves was thin cotton gloves. The second set was rubber just like what we used for dishwashing at home. In the changing/dress out area, I would have on a one-piece bathing suit under my clothes so that when I removed my street clothes and placed them in the locker, my body was still covered. The Reactor Building and Auxiliary Building, where I usually performed the QC Inspections, were very warm. None of the plant structures were air conditioned. The bathing suit made good sense to me for modesty.

The dress out area was coed. In other words, both male and female workers shared the same lockers and dress out area. I don't think they ever dreamed a woman would be working at the power plant and would require access to the same areas as the maintenance personnel—mechanics, electricians, and Instrument & Control (I&C) technicians. Some of these guys liked to take advantage of the situation and make me see things I shouldn't have had to see. They would take their sweet time about changing into the radiation control clothing. At least that was the case when I was around. What a sight! I would do everything I could to ignore them: keep my back to the guys while I put on the overalls and sit on the bench with my head down without chatting to anyone while I put on the gloves and booties. This did not stop the guys from sometimes strutting around in their birthday suits.

I never complained about the conditions I had to work under. I knew that would just make matters worse. I had a good-paying job in a man's world and just figured this was the price I had to pay for being a part of it. For maybe two years I had to put up with the men strutting around in the changing area, for two years I ignored them, and then management put a stop to the male exhibition program. I think we got a female HP technician, and she DID say something.

By the end of my first year on site, I felt like I had gained the respect of my coworkers, management, and the maintenance personnel. I was no longer the "token female" they were required to have to satisfy the affirmative action goals. They knew I could do the job, did it well, and did it faster and better that the other QC Inspectors. At least, that's how I felt, and I was proud of all the inspection training and certifications I had secured. By the end of the second year, I was also the only QC Inspector with the American Welding Society (AWS) structural inspector certifications along with the mechanical, electrical, and I&C certifications. Life was good.

That year Jerry showed up at the plant in the engineering group as a contract mechanical engineer. He was maybe five feet, eight inches tall, with dark hair, dark eyes, and olive skin. He was so charming, handsome, and sweet! I met him in the Auxiliary Building one day. He was performing a preventative maintenance test on a Feedwater Pump, and I was performing an inspection required by one of the work packages. We started dating that weekend.

Up until that point, I had been so busy working, training, and fixing up the house with the girls that I did not give a boyfriend a second thought. Frances and Melanie were in school and seemed to enjoy everything about Crystal River—our home, our church, and our weekend trips. Most weekends we would travel to one of the beautiful freshwater springs in north or central Florida. One weekend we even took an airboat ride over the salt flats near Crystal River. It was amazing! I had the upper deck with the driver, and Frances and Melanie were buckled into the lower seats. Apparently, they did not see much from their viewpoint, and all the bugs, flies, and critters in the tall grasses came into the boat on the lower level as we raced through the flats. Airboats are loud when the jet engine is running, and the driver and I had ear muffs on. I was having a fabulous time, and we never heard all the screaming from below. Those girls looked horrible when we finally finished the ride, and they were mad as hornets. Bugs, grasshoppers, and dragonflies in their hair, teeth…everywhere! Fear had completely enveloped their bodies because neither could move for a moment when we stopped, and their eyes were as big as saucers.

Jerry and I started spending a lot of time together. He preferred his place on the river in Homosassa, and initially, I did also. But he never invited the girls. He wanted me to himself, he would say. Fortunately, I had great neighbors and babysitters to help me with Frances and Melanie by then. He and I would travel to Key West in South Florida and to Canada, New York, and Philadelphia. He was so much fun, and he was getting serious about our relationship. He had taken me to meet his family, had given me a beautiful diamond necklace, and was hinting about marriage. The vision he had was that I would leave my job and that the girls and I would travel with him. Even with all the joy he brought me, I did not share the same loving feelings that he had for me. Plus, I loved my job, my neighborhood, and my church. Frances and Melanie seemed to be an afterthought for him. He avoided bringing the girls along wherever we went, even the weekends at his place. I attributed the need for privacy to his desire for intimacy. As a young woman in my mid to late twenties, he suited my needs perfectly. That is, until I realized I was pregnant.

Now what do I do? I thought. I knew if I told him, he would be able to persuade me to marry him, leave my job, and put him first and foremost in my life. My heart was not ready for the commitment, and it weighed on me greatly that he did not seem to connect, or care to nurture a relationship with my girls. Would they always be second fiddle to this child of his? So many things went through my mind. Finally, I spoke to my regular OB/GYN doctor, and he told me about the abortion clinic in Gainesville, Florida, near the college. It just seemed like the right thing to do. Everything would be confidential, I could keep my job at the power plant, the girls would stay the priority for me, and it would be one less mouth to feed. How in the world could I handle another child in my life? Even though I was making good money as a QC Inspector, it seemed like I was always struggling financially.

So, I justified in my self-centered egotistical mind breaking up with Jerry and aborting the child. I did not ask the Lord to guide me; I relied solely on my own selfish deductive reasoning with no input from my church associates, local pregnancy center, or family. Scripture says, "Come near to God and he will come near to you…" (Jas. 4:8), but I did not draw on the Lord's wisdom as I should have.

By that time, I was working with my friend Sam at the plant, and he lent me the fifteen hundred dollars required for the procedure in Gainesville. Medical insurance would not cover the cost of abortions. Even if insurance did, I would never have used it for fear someone would find out what I did. I was ashamed that I had let myself get pregnant and felt trapped. I kept saying to myself that it was perfectly acceptable and that I had the right to do as I pleased with my body and the pregnancy. It was the mid-1980s, after all! Women such as I were making great progress and advancement in areas that had always been limited to men in the past. Also, to expect the other QC Inspectors to take on more responsibilities because I was pregnant would have been humiliating. They would be so mad at me! Plus, an unmarried woman having a baby was unheard of in that time. I would embarrass myself, my family, and my daughters. I felt alone, ashamed, and scared and was determined to be successful in the job I had.

The clinic never mentioned any options in lieu of an abortion (such as adoption). They did not try to persuade me otherwise. Of course, in their defense, I came in asking for an abortion. The nurse administered a sedative, and just like with your OB/GYN exam, you are put in stirrups with your legs open. The abortion doctor then vacuumed out the baby. I could not see what he was doing, but I could hear the vacuum. There was tugging here and there on my uterus. The process, beginning to end, took maybe fifteen minutes.

Sam had taken me to the clinic and took me back home afterwards. I cried because my heart was broken. I knew afterwards what I did not know before, that my heart would ache terribly for the innocent life I had destroyed. But I kept justifying, even then, over and over in my selfish mind, that it was what had to happen under the circumstances. To keep from going insane, I would bury that memory for years deep in my subconscious mind.

I would later learn that failure, consuming fear, and shame are not of God, but of Satan. God only gives you and me love, grace, hope, and assurance. Because God hates sin, His Son, the Lord Jesus Christ, became sin for our salvation. You and I can have everlasting life only because of His Son and His death on the cross. He took our sins away forever. The Scripture says, "Have mercy on me, O God, according to your unfailing love; according to your great compassion blot out my transgressions. Wash away all my iniquity and cleanse me from my sin" (Ps. 51: 1–2).

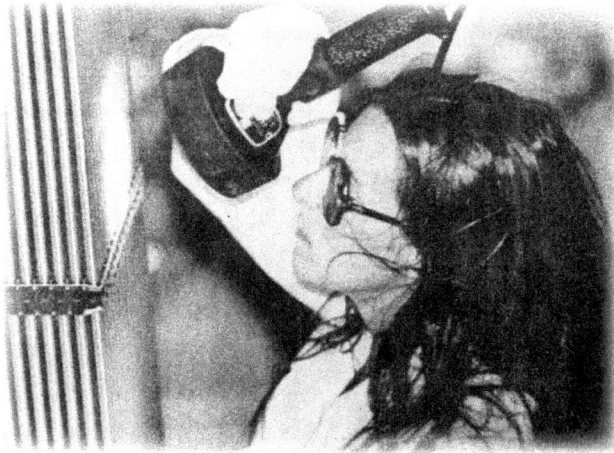

Deborah in Crystal River, Florida, Inspecting a Nuclear Fuel Assembly, 1981

Project Manager and Sam

*A*fter a three-day weekend, I hit the ground running. I needed a new focus and got it. I had been recently promoted and was now performing Project Manager duties. In 1984, at the power plant, I was responsible for eighty million dollars' worth of plant repairs, maintenance, and system modifications. I had a new challenge and focus, and my girls would be fine. I was convinced that these opportunities would not have presented themselves had I announced an unscheduled pregnancy out of wedlock. You see, it was still a man's world I was working in, and the opportunities went to the strong, hardworking, and determined. At least that was how I felt at the time, with little remorse for my attitude and actions. It was done; it was behind me. I had to move on.

The power plant system modifications I was responsible for were based on the Three Mile Island Nuclear Plant accident in 1979 and were now being installed during the 1985 and 1987 outages. The time delay between the plant accident and the installation had everything to do with the design, manufacturing, and testing of the new systems prior to installation on site. Sam was my lead engineer and contractor for the Reactor Vessel maintenance, with duties that included the core barrel bolt inspections and replacement, if needed. The Reactor Vessel supplier had determined that the material they used for the core barrel bolt original design and fabrication in the late sixties and seventies was susceptible to stress corrosion cracking. "Stress corrosion cracking" was a metallurgical term used to describe a failure mechanism. The Crystal River Nuclear Plant was the first plant to have the bolts ultrasonically tested to see if the engineering concern was warranted. If defects were found, the challenging task of bolt replacement would be required on the irradiated vessel with remote handling tools. Only the inspection activity was in the outage schedule. That meant any bolt changeout activity was Critical Path. The Critical Path designation is assigned to tasks whereby, each hour each day, work is performed beyond the schedule of inspection, extending the outage by the same amount of time. It also means the company is losing one million dollars each day in revenue by not generating electricity for sale to the public. It is a very stressful position for a Project Manager and her team to be in. Sam had become a close friend, a confidant, and a technical expert to guide me on many of the repairs and modifications.

Sam was six feet, four inches tall, with very fair skin, straight, brown, gray-streaked hair to his shoulders, and a mustache. I respected his technical and social abilities greatly, even though his tobacco chewing annoyed me. He was also a married man. The team respected Sam as their technical leader—he was one of the "good ole boys"—and that made my task as the manager much easier.

The bolts of interest were holding the Reactor Vessel internal components together and housed the nuclear reaction fuel assemblies during operations. Therefore, the vessel, the bolts, and everything around these components was highly radioactive. At all times, the internal components, such as the core barrel, had to be kept underwater. The barrel was maybe twenty feet tall and twelve feet in diameter, and once we removed it from the reactor vessel, we set it on a stand designed for this purpose in the deep end of the pool. At all times during the lift and repositioning, the vessel was covered with water. Once set, we positioned a work platform on top of the vessel for personnel and tool access to support the inspections. Personnel working on the platform, including Sam and I, wore protective clothing and radiation monitors at all time. The protective clothing for this job was double plastic boots on our feet, full body white cotton coveralls, and cotton and rubber gloves on each hand. Masking tape sealed the area between boots and coveralls on the legs and sealed the sleeve and glove area on each arm. A white cotton hood was required on your head, and any item, such as a tool, taken into the work area was tied off in one fashion or another.

To access and inspect the bolts around the core barrel, we used long handling tools with ultrasonic transducers on the end. The transducer was lowered into position and placed on the bolt head to verify the bolt's ten-and-a-half-inch length was fully intact. If the ultrasonic measurement was ten and a half inches in length, then the bolt was serving its purpose and was structurally sound. Unfortunately, we immediately discovered that many of the bolt heads were partially cracked and even, in some cases, completely severed off. A welded lock tap on top of each bolt held the severed bolt head in place. Had the welded lock tap not been used, these two-and-a-half-inch bolt heads would have been discovered much earlier as they bounced around the reactor vessel and primary coolant system, potentially causing considerable damage. The Core Barrel Bolt work, which I was responsible for managing, was now Critical Path with an unknown completion date. This was a "first of a kind' industry issue with no procedures to follow. It was several weeks before we relinquished that Critical Path classification.

Sam was such a blessing to me and the girls throughout the long days and short nights during that ordeal. He would take the girls to school events when I was tied up and feed them dinner. Frances and Melanie loved Sam. I was beginning to love him too. But even with all the kindness, helpfulness, and sweet consideration,

I had to keep foremost in mind the fact that he was a married man. Albeit not happily married, he was still a married man with no divorce intent. Back in Lynchburg, VA, his children lived with his wife, and he loved his children dearly. With all the time we spent together at work, and in the evenings planning and scheduling, it just came natural to my evil flesh to take that next step in the relationship and sleep together.

It wasn't long before I realized I was pregnant, again. I was doing so well with my career, caring for my girls, paying for our first home, and had even saved a few dollars. How in the world could I be so careless and stupid a second time?

I never even considered keeping the baby since I had the option to abort. Again, I never spoke to the Lord about what I should do. I never sought His guidance as a good Christian always should. My selfish self, again, just knew what was best for me, my career, and my family. All these things were much more important to protect than this unborn child. At least, I thought so at the time...later I came to realize that I had been a coward. Instead of seeing the baby as a blessing from God and an opportunity to affect change in how women could be treated and accommodated at the power plant, I relied on my wisdom, not God's. The flesh is weak, so Satan can control our lives—if we let him. And Satan was in complete control of me as I stayed self-centered and determined. Other than Sam, I consulted no one about the circumstances. When I made an appointment at the abortion clinic, again, I was never encouraged to consider other options. The abortion clinic in Gainesville just did what I asked them to do.

Sam took me to the abortion clinic to abort the baby. I was about three months along. Again, my heart ached, and I cried. Again, I was ashamed, scared, and fully realized how weak and controlling my flesh was.

Sam and I worked together three years through two outages, and then he went back to his home in Virginia.

Deborah in Crystal River, Florida,
Project Manager for
Turbine De-Stack/Re-Stack, 1984

Career, Joseph, and Grandchildren

*M*y career with Florida Power Corporation flourished. After the Core Barrel bolt outage and the demonstration of my Project Manager skills, I was given a twenty percent raise, apparently the most anyone at the time had ever been given in one year. The company continued to give me every opportunity to succeed and prosper. So, in 1986, when I met Joseph, an electrical engineer and Fossil Power Plant Superintendent, I was smitten. He was working for me, just like Sam had, as a technical consultant. I oversaw the plant High Pressure Turbine Rotor de-stack and re-stack, and he was to tell me which maintenance and modifications would be required on the electrical components, the turbine generator, and the exciter. Three years later, in 1989, we were married and stayed together for fifteen wonderful years.

During the time Joseph and I were married, my oldest daughter Frances met and married her college sweetheart in 1997. A couple of years later, on November 10th, with this proud new grandma in the delivery room, I observed the birth of my first grandchild, Deborah Ann. It was, without a doubt, one of the most profound occasions of my life. At that very moment, God revealed to me the miracle of birth and what I had done when I killed my babies. I had selfishly cut their lives short before they even had a chance to breathe, live, and love. They never saw the light of the world. I gave up their smiles, warmth, love, and even the grandchildren they would have given me one day. Those selfish acts in the 1980s, which I had suppressed as "justified under the circumstances," came back to haunt me.

Ever since 1972, when my mother-in-law had insisted that I accept the Lord as my Savior and get baptized before I married her son David, throughout my career at power plants, and when I was married to Joseph, I attended church. Not because I felt I had to, but because I wanted to. I always found nourishment with each visit, a positive energy, and as I got older, I made more connections in my mind between biblical wisdom and dealing with the struggles in today's world.

One Sunday, not long after my grandchild was born, as the preacher taught from the Old Testament about the Ten Commandments, I was analyzing my compliance with each Commandment. I had done pretty good with Not Taking the Lord's Name in Vain, but needed to improve. I did pretty good with Loving my Neighbor as Myself, but needed to improve. I had honored and obeyed my dear Momma and Daddy, for the most part. But, when it came to Thou Shalt not Kill, my jaw dropped, and I gasped for air. I realized at that moment that I was a Murderer. A Cold-Blooded Killer. The shame and guilt were almost overwhelming as I set in the church pew, and my heart ached for the babies I had killed. It physically hurt me to realize what I had done to my babies, myself, and to my God and His Son, Jesus Christ. Neither the Lord nor those babies ever had a say in my decision, and that's where I was wrong. I'm sure Satan was smiling and extremely pleased with the self-centered actions I had taken.

Jesus says in John, "Then you will know the truth, and the truth will set you free" (Jn. 8:32). That afternoon, once I was safely home in my private space, I finally knew and acknowledged the truth of my sin as I got on my knees and asked the Lord to forgive me. I cried as I reconstructed for Him what I had done, why I thought it was the right thing to do under the circumstances, and how I now realized it was not the right thing to do. I had no right to take the life of God's children. What of the families who would have loved them? What of the fathers who I never even asked if they wanted the child to raise? What of their God-given right to a life? I knew I had been playing God instead of listening to Him.

God, through His love and grace, accepted and forgave me. He promises in His Word, "For I will forgive their wickedness   and will remember their sins no more" (Heb. 8:12). The Holy Spirit continues to reveal the truth of this Scripture to my spirit and continues to remind me that I am truly forgiven.

Then, years later, God told me to write this book.

**Deborah with First Grandchild,
Deborah Ann, Crystal River, Florida, 2000**

Love and Grace

*W*hy should you care about aborted babies? Why should you care about the psychological impact of these decisions on the mother? Why should you care that someone you love may be making the worst mistake of their life? Why should you care that a father never got to know and love a child who was his own flesh and blood? Why should you care that a loving, childless couple has begged the Lord for the blessing of that child you killed?

Every single year, more than 900,000 babies are aborted in the USA. That's at least 900,000 women each year who are forever scarred by the decision to abort and who are potentially changed physiologically by the experience. In World War I and World War II combined, 522,000 US men and women died saving our country from tyranny. Yet today, in the USA, we give a doctor permission and legally kill more than 900,000 innocent babies a year! Annually, 41 million are killed worldwide. How and when did we become so barbaric as to kill our own and be so accepting of murder?

Like me, women who have chosen to abort may wonder what that child could have been, what they would have accomplished if they were born and given a chance. As I get older, I miss the whole lineage of that child, such as lost grandbabies. I miss the joy and God-given love they would have provided to my family and this precious country of ours.

Think long and hard before you make the decision to abort your baby. Pray to the Lord our God for guidance, and allow Jesus and the Holy Spirit to show you the right way. And, if it's your friend who is considering an abortion, pray with her, ask the Lord to guide her, and stay by her side as Satan tries his best to take that precious life from her. Satan and his evil, self-centered friends will make an abortion sound so appealing. He will show women many reasons to protect their career and their freedom and will encourage them to keep the pregnancy a secret and abort the child. In the Bible, Jesus commands Paul to minister to the lost, "To open their eyes and turn them from darkness to light, and from the power of Satan to God, so that they may receive forgiveness of sins and a place among those who are sanctified by faith in me (Jesus)" (Acts 26:18). Likewise, we should do everything we can to pour light into the lives of our hurting sisters and point them to Jesus.

If you're facing an unplanned pregnancy, seek out a Christian Pregnancy Center for guidance. Use the internet search engine to find "Pregnancy Center nearby," or go to www.care-net.org and put in your city and zip code. These wonderful folks will guide you in the options. They typically provide free pregnancy tests, adoption guidance, and ultrasound examinations so you can see your baby, and they will help if you suspect you could have contracted a sexually transmitted disease (STD). They will educate you on the choices you can make that are biblical, ethical, loving, and best for you and your child. Most of the facilities/pregnancy centers have a baby supply program to help with food and with clothing your baby.

In the Scripture, Jesus says, "For everyone who asks receives; the one who seeks finds; and to the one who knocks, the door will be opened" (Matt. 7:8). Ask the Lord to lead you, and listen to His instructions. REALLY listen. Remember, God can read your inner thoughts and your heart, and He knows your wants and needs. He knew you before you were born! He knew you in the womb. Satan cannot read your thoughts, your heart, or your needs. Satan only knows what you verbalize or write in correspondence. Be careful what you say and document…always. Satan will use your own weaknesses to trap you.

And if you know mothers who have aborted their children, remember do not judge, for you will be judged. The Scripture says, "Do not judge, and you will not be judged. Do not condemn, and you will not be condemned. Forgive, and you will be forgiven" (Lk. 6:37).

Only by the grace of God through His Son Jesus, who died for you and me, can I forgive myself for killing my babies. Please learn from my mistakes, and do not have an abortion. If you have had an abortion like me and are feeling the shame and guilt of this decision, PRAY. Seek the Lord and His forgiveness. Ask the Lord to save you, recognize Jesus was born of a virgin, died for our sins, rose on the third day, and has ascended to Heaven, where He sits at the right hand of our Father, God. The Bible says, "If we confess our sins, he is faithful and just and will forgive us our sins and purify us from all unrighteousness" (1 Jn. 1:9). Ask Jesus to forgive you and allow the Holy Spirit to guide you in every decision from that day forward. You and I have everlasting life only because Jesus died for our sins. Even the sin of killing our babies.

Background Information and Recent Statistics to Consider

- In 1973, the U.S. Supreme Court's *Roe v. Wade* decision legalized abortion. It was already legal in some states, but the decision by the Supreme Court imposed a uniform framework for state legislation. Since 1973, in the USA alone, more than 60 MILLION babies have been aborted (www.numberofabortions.com). With the current population of 325 million, that means that since 1973, about 20 percent of our citizens have been murdered by their mothers.

- The leading cause of death in 2018 was the aborting of 41 million babies worldwide. There are more deaths from abortion than from all deaths from cancer, malaria, HIV/Aids, smoking, alcohol, and traffic accidents combined. (Thomas D. Williams, www.breitbart.com/health/2018/12/31/abortion-leading-cause-of-death-in-2018-with-41-million-killed)

- Globally, just under a quarter of all pregnancies (23 percent) were ended by abortion in 2018, and for every 33 live births, 10 infants were aborted. (Thomas D. Williams, www.breitbart.com/health/2018/12/31/abortion-leading-cause-of-death-in-2018-with-41-million-killed)

- A full one-third of the population in the USA is missing since 1973 due to abortion. (Dr Edward G. Austen, Jr. Pro-Life 101 Session One, www.care-net.org)

- Four out of 10 women who had an abortion were actively attending church at the time of their abortion. (Dr Edward G. Austen, Jr. Pro-Life 101 Session One, www. care-net.org)

- According to New York's abortion report, there were 82,189 abortions performed on New York residents in 2016. Out of the 47,718 total reported pregnancies experienced by non-Hispanic black women, almost half— 49 percent—ended in abortion, and 47 percent made it out of the womb alive. That's more black babies aborted than born alive in New York. (Patrina Mosley, CP Op-Ed Contributor, January 30, 2019, www.christianpost.com/voice/new-york-and-planned-parenthood-a-eugenic-match-made-in-heaven.html)

- According to a recent Marist poll, 75 percent of Americans believe that abortion should be limited to within the first three months of pregnancy. This number also includes more than 6 in 10 (61 percent) who identify as "pro-choice" on abortion. (Patrina Mosley, CP Op-Ed Contributor, January 30, 2019, www.christianpost.com/voice/new-york-and-planned-parenthood-a-eugenic-match-made-in-heaven.html)

- Seven states (now eight with New York) plus Washington, DC, already have no gestational limits on abortion. The seven states include Alaska, Colorado, New Hampshire, New Jersey, New Mexico, Oregon, and Vermont. (Melissa Barnhart, CP Reporter, January 30, 2019, www.christianpost.com/news/7-states-already-allow-abortion-up-to-birth-not-just-new-york.html)

Author's Afterword

*A*re you pregnant right now? Are you a woman contemplating an abortion? The Lord is trying to talk to you, and He put this book in your hand. Just as He has told me to speak against abortion, the Lord God, His Son, and the Holy Spirit have put you and me together today for a reason. It's not a coincidence. If you have read my story, you know that I had two abortions. So I understand your situation. And what I want you to know is that abortion is not the answer. Abortion is sin…and sin always brings destruction. I wish I could go back and undo what I have done. But I can't. God has indeed forgiven me, but I want to help you avoid this trap. Abortion may be the easy way in the short-term, but it is not the path you want for you and your baby.

PLEASE don't think of your baby as some sort of inanimate object. Your baby is alive. He/she is a person. Scripture says, "When Elizabeth heard Mary's greeting, the baby leaped in her womb, and Elizabeth was filled with the Holy Spirit. In a loud voice she exclaimed, "Blessed are you among women, and blessed is the child you will bear" (Lk. 1:41–42). These verses illustrate the *person* that lived in Elizabeth's womb.

The timing of your pregnancy may not be the best, but your pregnancy can result in good. Scripture says, "And we know that in all things God works for the good of those who love him, who have been called according to his purpose" (Rom. 8:28). God has a plan for you and your baby right now. Let your heart fill with courage and love, not hatred, for this child, your child, who has the potential to bring you great joy, love, and maturity. Despite the circumstances, your baby is a precious gift from God with a purpose. Scripture says, "For you (GOD) created my inmost being; you knit me together in my mother's womb. I praise you because I am fearfully and wonderfully made; your works are wonderful, I know that full well" (Ps. 139:13, 14). The key is to get right with God and align your will with His.

Find a quiet place you can be alone, or with a trusted Christian—at home, at church, in your car, or on a serene park bench where you can just sit, pray, and listen. Truly PRAY, be still, and ask the Lord God through His Son, Jesus, to guide you before you take a pill to flush the embryo from your womb or schedule an abortion. God will show you the way, but you must listen and be patient, trusting Him and Him alone for wisdom and guidance. When you truly trust in the Lord, His loving kindness will surround you, and you will feel His presence. Fear and anxiety will be replaced by love. Scripture says, "Come near to God and he will come near to you" (Jas. 4:8).

Before this pregnancy, you were a gift from God to your mother and father. Now you, or the adopting parents, have the same opportunity to love and cherish a precious baby like your mother loved and cherished you. Think back on the joy your birth would have brought to your family, and then focus on the joy your baby will bring everyone, especially you. Satan may be telling you this baby will bring nothing but financial burdens, will destroy job advancement opportunities, or will take away the freedoms you have today. The very opposite is true. Your baby will give you confidence and drive you have never felt before. Employers, nowadays, respect and admire someone who can balance family and their job responsibilities, and your freedoms are expanded, not taken away. Now picture that beautiful son or daughter walking by your side for the rest of your life or with their loving adoptive parents.

Resources

CARE NET

Founded in 1975, Care Net is a non-profit organization that supports one of the largest networks of pregnancy centers in North America and runs the nation's only real-time call center providing pregnancy decision coaching.

Go to the www.care-net.org search feature and put in your town name and zip code. They maintain a list of Christian Pregnancy Centers for your use.

Normal office hours:
Monday-Friday, 9:00 a.m.-5:30 p.m., EST.

44180 Riverside Parkway
Suite 200
Lansdowne, Virginia 20176

Phone: 703.554.8734
Fax: 703.554.8735
info@care-net.org

NATIONAL RIGHT TO LIFE

National Right to Life was founded in 1968 and is the nation's oldest and largest pro-life organization. NRLC works through legislation and education to protect innocent human life.

Go to www.nrlc.com and click on "Pregnant?" You can click on the Option Line link to find a Pregnancy Resource Center near you, or peruse the many resources available including legislation, statistics, myths, news, and guidance during a crisis pregnancy situation.

Call the toll-free hotline 24/7, 365 days of the year: (800) 848-LOVE

PROLIFE ACROSS AMERICA

PROLIFE Across America is a non-profit, non-political organization dedicated to changing hearts and saving babies' lives since 1989.

Go to prolifeacrossamerica.org and click on "Pregnancy Help." There are many resources listed that can give you the most helpful information and guidance on the next steps to take.

Call the hotline at 1 (800) 366-7773 to speak with a trained and educated counselor.

PO Box 18669
Minneapolis, MN 55418

www.ingramcontent.com/pod-product-compliance
Lightning Source LLC
Chambersburg PA
CBHW052104270326
41931CB00012B/2878